I am
Lucille Ball

BRAD MELTZER

illustrated by Christopher Eliopoulos

DIAL BOOKS FOR YOUR READERS an imprint of Penguin Group (USA) LLC

I am **Lucille Ball.**

When I was a little girl, my mother tried to dress me in ribbons and bows.

But I was different from other girls.

My idea of fun was horsing around with my dad.

He used to throw me up to the ceiling, always catching me and making me laugh.

When I was three years old, the local grocer used
to let me put on a show at his store.
My favorite was this frog routine.

Customers paid me with pennies and candy,
making these my first professional appearances!

I had even more fun when my aunt used to let me work in her beauty salon.
She'd let me do the hair of her customers' children.

Soon after, the beauty salon went out of business.

But my childhood wasn't all goofiness and games.
When I was seven years old, I went to live with Grandmother Peterson.
She didn't like the way I played.
In fact, she thought having fun was a bad thing.

Instead, in her dark kitchen, she made me wash lots of dishes.

She didn't even allow any mirrors in her house, except for one in the bathroom.

She thought they made you think too much of yourself.

When I rode on trolley cars, I used to make silly faces at my reflection. Try it. You'll see so many possibilities.

To Grandmother Peterson, little girls weren't supposed to be bold, sassy, or silly.

As punishment, she'd send me to bed before sundown.

I still remember lying there, hearing all the other kids playing outside.

But no matter how tough those days were, I had one thing to get me through it:

My sense of humor.

On rainy days, I'd play on the back porch and make dolls out of clothespins. I gave them all personalities.

You wouldn't believe the adventures we had.